Staying And Standing Women

Staying And Standing Women

BY

Cheryl Leitschuh, Ed.D.

eBookstand

http://www.career-future.com

Published By
eBookstand
http://www.ebookstand.com
Division of CyberRead, Inc.
Mukilteo, WA USA 98275
1794_1

ISBN: 1-58905-132-9

Printed in the United State of America.

Preface

This book is written to celebrate the "Standing and Staying" power of women. It is not to say that men do not have this capacity but it is to suggest that it is different for women than for men.

Let me tell you about how the concept for this book began. I was attending a Spiritual Retreat on "Being a Contemplative Woman." The facilitator/guide for the retreat was very thought provoking as he shared stories of women from the Bible. One session revolved around being a "Standing and Staying" woman. Two stories I remember were first of the women at the crucification. It was the women that took Jesus from the cross and brought him to the tomb. There was no fear of their own persecution instead they did what they needed to do despite possible consequences to self.

The other story was of the women who were on the journey with the Israelites to find the promised land. Every night they would build a fire and dance and sing. The men said, "How can you do this? We have no clue where we are, where we are going or if we will be killed tonight. How can you celebrate?" The women said, "This is the only moment I am certain of, so why not celebrate?"

From this retreat I felt compelled to tell the stories of modern day "Standing and Staying" women. Women who have forged ahead despite the challenges they face. Not necessarily miraculous women who are seen in a national spotlight. Rather women who have stood by, in an often quiet way, to move life forward in a positive direction and yet, only knowing they could count on today.

The stories you will read are wide and vary. They may be the stories of people the storyteller has known or stories of themselves. It includes spouses telling of their wife, children telling of their mothers, mothers of their children, friends telling of friends . . .. It makes no difference. They are all standing and staying women.

My hope for the reader is you will find comfort, wisdom and direction in valuing the life you lead and the impact you have on others. Not from the miracles you perform rather from the faith you bring to life every day.

--Cheryl Leitschuh--

Table of Contents

1

Healing Ourself While Healing Our Family

Story Submitted by: Doreen Johnson

The person I chose to tell you about is Susen Fagrelius. At a training ceremony, she received a call from her husband, saying that her daughter was in the hospital. Her daughter went through a day of excruciating pain and testing, and finally an emergency surgery. She was 16 or 17, and Susen was over a 1,000 miles away from home. I was privileged to watch her make decisions and to support her.

Most of us would have panicked and fled home. But Susen seemed to know that spiritually she was connected with her daughter and she could support her healing over this long distance. It was the most faith-based thing I've every experienced.

When she came home, there were several operations and challenges. They found out almost a week later what the pathology report said--dysgerminoma, a relatively rare form of ovarian cancer. So there was uncertainty, and a decision always to "see" Helen whole and healthy, and not to give any energy to fear. She asked for support from the community. She was very clear that her primary focus was on her daughter's health, her family's health and her health. She committed herself to what was needed in the moment.

They came through the healing process and her daughter is healthy once again. They celebrated the by holding a Ceremony For Life right after Thanksgiving. They invited all the people that had supported the family and Helen to a party to celebrate her life.

The incredible nature of her story is her courage and strength. She concentrated on her self-care enough to also give all she had to her daughter. She was able to create what was needed to guide and heal.

Susen is a very passionate woman. She saw this as healing for herself and her family. She was very clear that she was at war with the disease but that the war would be won by focusing on wholeness and beauty.

2

Strong Foundations

Story submitted by: Candace Mailand

"I believe that Jesus is the rock, the foundation from which all things come, and he worked through them to provide me with a strong foundation in life."

The two women that I wanted to talk about are my grandmother, June Graves and my mother, Penny Moehn. These two women projected a true celebration of life. They challenged adversity head-on and despite the many obstacles they encountered in life, they always persevered and overcame. We say that the Lord only puts as much on our plate as we can handle, but I think – many times - their plates overflowed.

My grandmother, born in 1916, was always a working woman. She married in her late 20's, which in those days was almost unheard of. Her attitude was that she was having too much fun to worry about getting married. After she married my grandfather, she continued to work, side-by-side with him. They had a women's retail clothing/dry goods business. My grandfather had been in the war and had developed many illnesses. My grandmother became the caretaker for him and her mother who eventually came to live with them. Along with this she raised two children, worked a full time job, yet was always filled with such love of life.

After my grandfather passed away, my grandmother continued running the store by herself, tending to the buying, the accounting and the employee issues. When she eventually sold the store at age 66, she was bored stiff. This was a woman who could not sit down. So 3 years later she interviewed for a job in retail and went back to work full-time.

My grandmother had terrible rheumatoid arthritis in her hands and feet. They were very crippled—and it was so hard for her to get around. But she still got up every morning, put on her walking shoes, went to the gym and walked 5 miles. I remember her telling me, "The day I sit down is the day I die."

This incredible spirit carried over to my mom. My mom was 17 when I was born. My brother followed five years later. Soon after my brother's birth, my parents divorced and my mom found herself in the position of needing to find a job, caring for two small children and tending to all household responsibilities. It was not a good situation for her but she persevered. She raised my brother and I and worked full time. She worked from the ground up at a bank to eventually become a Vice President. .

My grandmother and mother were able to make friends for life. They were able to energize others, and inspire others to excel and rise above themselves. They treated people with respect, and at the same time, were not afraid to make those hard decisions. They are women with high ethical standards and integrity.

These two women were always there for me. They are my true inspiration in life. My grandmother's spirit remains strong. Although she has passed away, I find myself talking to her and asking her questions on a daily basis and in my heart, she answers back. Over the last 3 years, I've experienced two powerful dreams about her.

The first one came a year and a half after she passed away. Life was very challenging for me. I had a new position at work. I had a new baby and I was very overwhelmed in life with all my new responsibilities. I dreamt I was walking through a house. I opened a door and my grandmother was sitting there in a chair by a window. There was a soft glow in the room. My grandmother raised her arms to me. I went to her, knelt down and laid my head on her lap. I felt her brushing my hair and scratching my back. I had an overwhelming sense of peace. When I woke from the dream, I could smell her – her perfume – in my room. It was so real. That dream brought such a sense of peace, of comfort to me, knowing that she was telling me that she is always there with me.

The other dream happened recently. I had surgery for cancer about a year ago. I had a busy schedule of doctor's visits as well as another new position at work. Life was very busy, as it always seems to be anymore. In this dream I found myself on an operating table with people standing over me. I thought to myself, "Oh my gosh, I'm dead. They're preparing me because I'm dead." I remember looking to my right. There's a city scene in front of me. I thought to myself, "This is not how I imagined death to be. It's supposed to be this serene walk through a tunnel with a bright shining light to guide me. Where are my grandmother and my great grandmother? They should be meeting me. I know no one." The next thing I know, an elderly African American woman walks up to me with a twinkle in her eye. I asked her, "Have you seen my grandmother? I am waiting for my grandmother. She's to be here waiting for me." This little woman looked up and smiled at me and said, "How do you know she's not here? You need to look beyond what you see - to what really lies beneath, because there you'll find your answer." She was trying to send me a very strong message that we need to look within ourselves – beyond what we see with our eyes – to what really lies beneath. There we will find our answers. It was an incredibly powerful dream. I continue to reflect on both of these dreams and they continue to inspire and comfort me.

My mother and grandmother are spiritual people and I was raised to respect and feel God's presence in all I do, in all I am. They taught me to do what is 'right' and not to be swayed by the opinions of others. Despite all the adversity that they encountered in life, they had this incredible ability to renew themselves. They embraced change. They didn't fight against it. They would say, "This too shall pass." Their ability to constantly give of themselves without ever expecting anything in return. By doing so, they renewed themselves.

My mother has always made me believe that I am capable of doing anything that I want in life. I remember when I was very young, seven years old; my mother looked at me and said, "You need to learn that no one is going to take care of you in your life but you. We will always be here for you, but you need to be prepared to stand on your own, and that's what I'm going to prepare you for in your life." And she did. No matter what life has brought my way, I am able to stand on my own and face those things head on. After all, I am the daughter of Penny Moehn and the granddaughter of June Graves.

3

Being True To Yourself

Story submitted by: Colleen Watson

My whole "coming out" story is probably the most difficult part of my life. Most of the population doesn't have to go through the adversity of growing up gay in the 60's. Believing that you're going to hell because of it. By coming to terms with myself, and by dealing with all the adversity that went with it, I learned an awful lot about me and how to overcome and deal with taking risks. This experience has helped me to become a successful business owner.

This is the story of a little girl that liked all the other girls in 2nd grade, and thought that was normal. Then I started growing up and hit puberty and realized that I was different. You don't know because you live inside of yourself and I didn't realize that my feelings were considered bizarre. In fact, I had a girlfriend in 8th grade, and I remember going to a movie theater with her. I had curlers in my hair because we had to go to a church thing later that night. I was sitting with my arm around my girlfriend and this guy walked by and looked at me really strange. I didn't understand what I was doing wrong. I couldn't understand what he was staring at. I thought it was the curlers in my hair. That's the level of naiveté that I would have at that age, and then I started piecing it together and realized that I had feelings that I had to keep to myself. Then I had to try to force myself to fit in, knowing that I didn't fit in.

Teenage years you really try to be a part of the group. To know that you are not and you won't fit in causes you try to cover up in a number of different ways. Sometimes it was being tough, and seeing how much trouble I could get myself into. I think I spent ½ of 8th grade in detention hall. Then I started becoming a goodie-two-shoes, and hang out with the really smart kids. In fact, my peer group was the valedictorian and salutatorian of my high school class. I'm still friends with them today. I became really involved with church work, trying to be a good girl and avoid these awful feelings because I knew they were a sin.

Finally in 11th grade we were at a retreat, and we were all supposed to write down our sins. So I wrote down my sin of homosexuality. We were burning our sins in this little ashcan that we had at the retreat. I threw mine in and the paint of the wastebasket caught on fire, and the whole thing went up. I knew that my sin was the greatest sin of all. So I'm walking around with this feeling of "Oh my god. I really am going to go to hell."

I managed to get through those years, feeling very awkward and went to college. I meet a man, and we decide we're going to get married because I don't know what else I'm supposed to do. I'm not real crazy about the guy. He's in the Navy and it was safe to have this long-distance boyfriend. I finally broke up that relationship and gravitating towards people in college that I cared about. Years later, one of the men that was one of my dear friends had his name on one of the AIDS quilts.

I went out into the world, and decided that I better get married. I did get married and had a child, and stayed drunk for an awful long time. That was the only way I could cope with my feelings. All the time trying to be something I'm not and put on this great performance. Finally, I get into sales, and do a great job in sales; the performance though is eating away at me. I divorce my husband, and tell my parents that I couldn't do this anymore. I remember my parents and a Lutheran minister sitting in the living room saying, "we love the sinner but not the sin." They could not accept who I was. So that was the last time that I talked to my parents for 12 years.

During those 12 years, I really thought my way through a lot of things. I stayed actively alcoholic, angry at the world, hating everything about it. I could still work and make money. I finally discovered that I couldn't go on with the drinking. I went through some very dysfunctional relationships and finally became sober.

That was my born again experience. My life was saved through AA. In my recovery, I realized that my family relationships weren't just the fault of my parents, that I played a part as well. I decided that I was going to treat them in a way that they really could feel good about me. I learned to care about myself. I also managed to get myself into a wonderful relationship with Mary, which was the healthiest thing I ever did. I was sober for a year, and became involved with a person who was my equal, spiritual, and cared about the same values. Eventually I invited my parents to come over to my house and have a meal with me. They came to my graduation for my master's degree and they also came to my open house for my new business. It was this driving to be accepted by the world was just trying to be accepted by my parents. When I finally accepted that they were doing the best they could. They probably really did care about me, and then they were able to overcome their feelings.

Today I am in many leadership activities and give back to the community in many ways. I am a church leader at St. Anne's Episcopal. I am a youth leader. I am a confirmation mentor. I am active in the worship service. I am in the healing ministry, where we offer prayers at the alter. I am active in the Rotary club. I've been past president, and I'm going to be back on the board next year. I am still involved on the alumni board at Augsburg College. I've been named an outstanding alumnus of the campus because of the work I've done with the college and reaching out to the students. I sing in the One Voice Community Chorus and I have been appointed to the governor's board of directors in the area of commerce. I have a fulfilling life with many friends, close family relations, a successful business, good health and much happiness. I guess you could say I am living the American dream.

4

Welcoming Women

Story Submitted by: Mary Marso-Schmitz

I've always marveled at my grandmother's ability to be welcoming. Grace Anderly had such a wonderful way of making people feel welcomed in her home. I think it's even more of a gift when you recognize that she did it with little or no money.

My grandma and grandpa married when my grandma was very young. They moved into the farmhouse that was his families. All of their married life, until my grandpa died, her two single sister-in-laws and a brother-in-law lived in the house. It was a small house. We would have Christmas dinners there and we would eat in shifts, because there were always so many people that came. There were only two main rooms in the main floor. With no running water or indoors plumbing. Yet it was a grand feast and everyone loved going to Grandma's house for Christmas. Everyone received a gift, and it always felt so special. It might have been a pair of socks, but Grandma always had a wrapped gift for every guest that came to her house. When people ask me where I got my smile, or my sense of entertaining, my Grandmother deserves the credit without a doubt.

Within the last year, when my granddaughters were visiting, it took me back to a time when I was baking chocolate chip cookies with my grandmother. Because chocolate chips were an expensive ingredient, we didn't have many chocolate chips in each cookie. It was my job to make sure that grandma got some in each cookie. I remember one day measuring ingredients with Grandma for cookies. Grandma paused said, "Mary Grace, 1/3 cup of brown sugar. How much is 1/3 cup?" Well, she was doing that as a lesson for me, in measurement, but I didn't understand that. In my mind, I remembered thinking, "poor Grandma. She doesn't even know what 1/3 cup is." She was just one of those people that never has been publicly recognized, but was a gift to her entire family.

My mother, Mary Irene Marso, was very bright and had no money. One of her aunts offered to send her to college. She received a two-year teaching degree at Mankato State, and graduated magna cum laude. She ended up married to my father, who had an eighth grade education. My mom was a very strong person. Since we had limited means, when I was about 10 or 11 years old, my mom went back to work at the local grocery store in order to pay our grocery bill. From that day forward, she worked in that grocery store and took over the management of the store.

There was a hermit that lived outside of town, and you rarely saw him. When you did it was from a distance, getting in or out of his car, or occasionally back off the road at his little place in the country. He would come into the grocery store that my mom worked in, and he would always come through at the alley entrance. My mom was always kind to him and took care of what he needed, so when she started working part-time, he made it a point of only coming in the days that my mother worked. After my mother had died, this man came to the Visitation, where there were a lot of people. For this man to risk being that public in coming to a mortuary, where there were so many people, was such a tribute to the person she was. For her, it was not about public recognition. It was about the joy of what kindness can do, and how uplifting it can be for people.

During the spring floods in Minnesota before Henderson had its dykes, it was not unusual to have, in the worst of floods, 1/3 to ½ of the town flooded. We lived up on the hill, so we weren't subject to being removed from our home, or having the flood invade our home. My family home had two bedrooms, which was very small. During the flood of '65, my mom and dad had 6 extra people living in the house. They were all students who had been forced out of their homes. Having grown up in such a little house, the sense of hospitality flowed through my mom as well. Even though we had the smallest house out of any of my friends, my siblings and myself had more overnight guests and slumber parties than any of our other friends in school. It was just accepted that anyone was welcomed to come home with you. It really didn't matter if you called ahead of time. Somehow there was always room at the table.

“A woman is like a teabag – only in hot water do you realize how strong she it.”

-Nancy Reagan-

5

Teaching Role Models

Story Submitted By: Mary Marso-Schmitz

I had a high school home economics teacher named Mrs. Swenby. She and her husband lived in LeSueur, a town six miles from Henderson. She gave me such a sense of how to put on a dinner party in home economics class that I will never forget how to how to do table settings.

She was a very strong mentor of mine. She recognized my talent to work with other people and manage situations. She encouraged me to run for state office for Future Homemakers of America when I was only a sophomore in high school. She, by her actions, served as my campaign manager - sending out letters to other people involved in the process and coaching me through the election preparation and process. Then I went to the state convention, went through the interviews, and became state historian. And she was there every step of the way and throughout my term of service. For the next year, I was invited to speak at various district conventions around the state. Mrs. Swenby and her husband spent so many Saturdays that year taking me all over the state so that I could speak in front of conferences and conventions, and they weren't compensated for it. It was their gift to me. I always sensed her strong belief in me. She let me know she knew that I could do anything I wanted to do. That's always been in the back of my mind—that reinforcement that she kept giving me about what I was capable of doing—don't be afraid to try that—it was a wonderful gift, and she didn't expect anything in return. All of my adult life, until she had to leave her home and live with her daughter out East, I would make a point, at least every six months, to visit her at her home. When I arrived, she would always have the table set for tea and we would have to have formal tea. It is a wonderful memory.

6

Business Women Role Models

Story Submitted By: Mary Marso-Schmitz

Leota Ester. She is a good friend of mine today. She's in her early seventies. About 3 years ago, she sold the staffing business that she founded when she was 56 years old. During the course of our business association, we became very good friends, and that is how I got to know parts of her story.

Leota was actually trained as a teacher. She had three daughters. Her husband was a journalist, and she followed him from place to place. She saw an opportunity in Appleton in the temporary help industry and decided to start her own firm when she was 56 years old. It was extremely important to her that she mentors young women. During her tenure of ownership she sought out people with natural talent and untapped potential, and encouraged them in every way she knew, to develop their talents. Many of them became her managers, and did an excellent job for her.

Over the years she grew her company and sold it, leaving herself in a financially secure position for her retirement years. While she still owned the business, she began renting a flat in London for six weeks every spring and she took on the delightful task of showing friends and family the sights and highlights of London. She also took all the key people who had worked with her on staff to London, at her own expense.

Leota is also very involved in giving back to the community. She is extremely philanthropic. The things she's done have not been to achieve notoriety; they simply represent a part of who she is and what is important to her. She's a problem-solver; people turn to her to get things done and she doesn't disappoint them.

I was shopping with Leota last summer and I bought my daughter-in-law a red purse. Leota told me the story of when she was a young girl, she went to visit her cousin and aunt and uncle.

Her uncle was a minister in a very conservative congregation. She was so proud of her new gray suit, red purse, and new red shoes. Her uncle had a fit, because she was wearing red shoes. He believed and expressed strongly that it was not proper. She was so taken back by the encounter with him at such a vulnerable age that she never owned a red purse or red shoes again. When told the story that day I said, "today's the day." We went over to the section where the purses were and I made sure that she bought a red purse that day. The next morning I was leaving. She had an interview with a local television station related to employment trends and such. She was getting ready to leave, and as I was going out to the car, she opened the door and waved her red purse and exclaimed, "I think today is my red purse day!"

This year Leota did not rent the flat in London. Today she is managing a new challenge of caring for her husband who is experiencing the beginning stages of an aging illness of which she is not yet ready to assign a name. She has taken on this new phase in life with a sense of peacefulness and acceptance that was not a part of her life earlier. Prior to this if there was any condition, any situation that needed changing (or she wanted it to change), she went after achieving the results with her full focus. Now, she sees this life situation as one over which she does not have the control so, as she shared with me recently, "I need to change the way I do things, I still have more changing I need to do." What a great lady! She is such a good example for women to follow.

“Don’t be humble. You’re not that great.”

-Golda Meier-

7

Death, Strength and Growth

Story submitted by: Nicole and Lynn Loosbrock

I've always considered myself weak. I'm a very emotional person. I cry a lot and express my emotions very openly. So I thought that I would deal with my brother's death the same way that I deal with everything else in my life. I found a totally new side of myself when my brother was sick and dying. I found strength that I didn't know I had. Aaron was 20 years old when he was diagnosed with leukemia and 22 when he died.

Near the beginning of his illness, I was sitting with Aaron during a very painful procedure, a spinal tap. I remember feeling like I was going to throw up. This powerful, noxious feeling came over me and I had to sit down to avoid being sick. There is such helplessness in watching someone you love suffer.

Aaron and I came to depend on each other. He depended on my company and my comfort, and I depended on his emotional strength and his love. I was the person who grabbed the bucket and washcloth when Aaron was gong to throw up, which he did at least six times a day for three months straight. I held his hand through countless bone marrow biopsies. And consequently, I was the one who got to laugh and reflect with him. Aaron gave me the gift of pure, unselfish love and the gift of feeling useful and needed.

I found I had a calm and a strength that helped me deal with whatever was thrown my way. In contemplating Aaron's death, I thought I would be a mess when he died. At some point, however, selflessness takes over and all you want is peace and an end to the suffering. After Aaron's death, a friend of mine asked if I would have him back on this earth for one day to talk, if it meant that he would be in the hospital. My reply was instantaneous: definitely not. Aaron was my best friend, and I wanted what was best for him. Suffering on this earth was not what he wanted or needed. I've always considered myself selfish, but this was one time when I was not. Love is a powerful motivator.

At the funeral I was sad, and very, very numb. I recognize that in retrospect, but didn't realize quite how numb I was at the time. Immediately after someone dies, you don't have time to grieve because you're ultimately there to comfort everyone else. The purpose of the wake, and even to some extent the funeral, isn't for the family as much as it is for others.

The main thing that I gleaned from Aaron's funeral was that he made a huge difference in this world. All 500 plus people that were at the church were a testimony to that fact. Chairs were set up outside the church for people who couldn't fit inside. People sat outside the church just to be there for Aaron and for our family. That was living proof that Aaron's life was not in vain.

My family walked into the church with the processional and I sat next to my mom in the front row. Dad was on the other side of her, and my 60 or so other relatives in attendance sat all around us. There were three eulogists. One was my Uncle Jim; the other two were like second fathers to Aaron. Aaron had many "second parents." He became a part of everyone's family. And when Aaron was dying, these other "families" put their lives on hold to be by his side.

I didn't cry during the funeral service until one particular song was played – "The Wind Beneath My Wings." Growing up, I received a lot of attention because I did things the way that society dictates they should be done. I excelled in school, participated in clubs and volunteering, and other such things. Aaron didn't do so well in school because it wasn't a priority for him. Hence, I got the "positive" attention and reinforcement, while he did not always get the same. Throughout my entire school experience, though, he was always there in the background, making sure that I did well – always my support and my best friend. What an incredible gift that was to me. And so, that's why I cried when they played the song.

To help Aaron when he was at his worst is the greatest honor I've ever had. He meant everything to me, so it wasn't a chore. It was a very personal gift to allow me to care for him. I was probably at the hospital more than anyone else, just because my parents had to work, and he felt very comfortable with me. It was deeply meaningful that he wanted me there.

Aaron was diagnosed shortly after I'd moved home to Jacksonville from Atlanta. I had returned home for a year to figure out what to do with my life. Thus, I was in town when he was diagnosed. When he went into remission, I felt that I needed to get on with my life. Had I waited around for him to get sick again, it would have seemed I had little faith in his recovery and future. I applied to Emory to the nursing school because I wanted to be able to do what Aaron's nurses had done for him. Of all of his healthcare team, the nurses made the greatest impact in Aaron's day-to-day life. They were the people that made Aaron feel comfortable. They were his friends. They cared for him as a uniquely special person.

I enrolled in Emory's nursing school. My parents were very supportive, and so was Aaron. I had promised Aaron that if anything happened to him, I would return home. And when he relapsed, I did just that. I was on my way to an exam, when my cell phone rang. Aaron said, "I just called to tell you that I love you." It was a weird call and I wondered what was going on; Aaron had been progressing well following his bone marrow transplant. I asked where he was, and he said he was in the hospital. I said, "What are you doing there?" He replied, "I'm checking in." Something was terribly wrong, yet I had to go from that conversation to take an exam.

When I called my Mom after the exam, she told me the cancer had returned, something that Aaron couldn't tell me himself. That day I withdrew from Emory and returned to Jacksonville. When I arrived, Aaron said, "I'm so glad you came back, Colie [my nickname]. I really need you here." Those were the only words I needed to hear.

From that point onward, my mission was to be available to Aaron in any way that I could. I advocated for him when no one else could. He was so nice to people. He couldn't tell them to leave the room because he thought it would hurt their feelings. So I took on the role of the enforcer when it was in his best interest. When not at work, I would sit with him for eight hours. I was employed at the hospital where he was a patient, so I would visit him on my breaks. We would have breakfast together on the mornings that I worked. The days I wasn't working, I was committed to be with him. We would watch movies and talk. It was very special. It wasn't always easy because you feel the need to get away after you've been in a hospital for so long.

I think the reason that I was able to meet his needs was because he helped me through that period. He was the providing my strength. When he was dying at the end of his journey, he told me, "You guys need to get on with your life. You've dealt with this long enough. It's time for you to move on. Tell Mom not to worry about me. God has a plan for me." So he was taking care of us. It was therapeutic to be with him. That's probably why I was able to be so strong; I had more therapy from him than anyone else! He fought so valiantly, yet I would not want him to endure such incredible suffering just so we could be with him; he wouldn't want that. I'd not wish that for anybody, much less my little brother.

(Lynn) I'll never forget that Friday evening at St. Luke's Hospital when the hematologist escorted Frank, Nicole, and me into the family room to tell us that the leukemia had returned. There had been no signs of it between November and April. Hours earlier we had been encouraged by a preliminary pathology report, indicating possible engraftment activity from the bone marrow transplant. The painful truth was that Aaron faced formidable odds: recurrent leukemia; an infected and hemorrhaging bladder; and no signs of engraftment to provide a new immune system and the manufacture of blood cells. We knew that short of a miracle, there was no long-term probability for survival. Aaron's physician was offering hope to prolong his life via three options. But for how long? And at the expense of more pain and suffering?

The hope for Aaron's recovery that we had nurtured for 15 months was shattered; each of us struggled with the reality of life without our precious Aaron. I vividly remember Nicole saying, "Let's go talk to Aaron. We know what his decision will be." I recall being inspired by my daughter who was prepared to say, it is time to let go. We can't impose upon Aaron our selfish wishes for him to remain with us, and we can't burden him with our grief. The process during the coming days was now inevitable. It was time for Aaron to take final control…and he did so, calmly and methodically. He knew that God was calling for him, and he was incredibly prepared for his death and life eternal.

(Nicole) He had been thinking about it for a long time.

(Mom) And praying. That facilitated our ability as parents to let go and allow Aaron to manage the process of his death. During the week of his death, it took great restraint to relinquish control and allow others access to him.

Though I let go, Nicole was the sergeant at the door, making decisions about who could visit and when. We have this huge, loving family that dropped everything to fly in from all over the country. They had supported us long distance for 15 months. Our family is extremely optimistic and has strong faith, so it was generally believed that Aaron would beat the leukemia and survive. Now as they arrived to say good-bye, they began to grieve. They all had an intense need to spend time with Aaron and hold his hand. Aaron supported every one of his family and friends in the most incredible way during the week of his death. Aaron died April 18, four days after his 22nd birthday.

(Nicole) I was impressed with Mom. She had to address the details. She talked directly and candidly with Aaron. Did he want to be cremated? Buried? What were his wishes for his funeral service? Aaron loved music; what music did he want? What did he want done with his ashes? I was impressed with my Mother's strength in being able to deal with all of that. She had suffered an incredible loss, yet moved forward efficiently in planning the funeral, with the help of family. But I'm just impressed that she was able to do all that she did.

(Mom) To be able to do that I realized I would have to put my grief aside for a while. I relied on activity, all the things that had to be done, to get through that period, including the three weeks following Aaron's death. I delayed my own grieving to help everyone else through the tough times. That's probably not uncommon among women.

Immediately following the funeral, I did two things that irritated both Frank and Nicole. First, there were tons of acknowledgements. I didn't just send a card, I wrote a personal note to everyone. I also went through Aaron's personal effects. I wanted to give things that were symbolic to his friends and cousins. Aaron had so many friends of all ages. I would sort through his things, looking at them, touching them, and often times writing a personal note to the recipient. The symbolism of the process helped me.

Throughout the summer we took wonderful trips that our caring friends and family extended to us. This was a great respite.

(Nicole) Mom's big thing is caring for herself by caring for others. When she cares for others, she cares for herself. I think it's the same thing for me. As for keeping Aaron's memory alive, she had parties for every person who supported us during Aaron's illness. She invited friends to dinner to thank them for their support. I think that was what Mom did to begin the healing process. She would talk in detail about everything and just relive it; for her, that was comforting.

(Mom) In the fall, I started this incredibly planned regimen of entertaining many who had supported us throughout Aaron's illness. We had small dinners and big parties, reminiscing about the lessons Aaron taught us.

I crashed a little in late October, early November. After the rash of parties ended, my grieving accelerated; I was forced to deal more directly with my loss and my emotions. That was rough for Frank. He watched helplessly as I experienced the process. Obviously he couldn't stop it, but sometimes felt anger and frustration because he couldn't take control and intervene. In the end, he'd comfort and support me, often times reminiscing and crying with me.

I recognized that this would be a life-long process. Grief is not something that will end on a particular date, closed and sealed away. A friend who had lost two daughters advised that the grieving never ends; you simply rebuild your life around your grief.

From Aaron we learned the joy of living every moment. He chose not to be victimized, angry, and bitter about his cancer and early death. Aaron learned to relish every moment fully. He may have just vomited, or gotten a dose of pain medication, but if there was something comical on television or in a movie, he would laugh freely and enjoy that moment. Aaron had a wonderful appreciation of humor. After months of being confined to the hospital, Aaron was granted a two-hour pass to go home to his bedroom. As he got out of the car in the driveway, he paused to marvel at the sound of a small cricket in the grass. Most of us fail to recognize the natural beauty and wonder that surrounds us.

After he died, we found in his wallet this saying: "This is the only day I have to live. Yesterday is gone, and no matter how I try, I cannot change it. Tomorrow is not yet here, nor do I know if it will ever come. Therefore, let me make the most of today." Aaron lived that philosophy. My nature has always been to plan, put a process in place, and make things happen. But that needs to be balanced with enjoying the moment and the beauty around us. That's one of the many things Aaron taught us.

We have a beautiful picture of Aaron running on the beach toward the surf on a sunny day, arms outstretched, seagulls flying all around him. He was probably 18 or 19 years old. It epitomizes him breaking free of his illness and his body that no longer served him. We duplicated this photo and attached a copy of the handwritten quote found in his wallet. We gave these to family and friends at Christmas. It's another way of keeping Aaron's memory alive and sharing some of the wisdom we gained from him.

We are not human beings trying to be spiritual. We are spiritual beings trying to be human.

-Jacquelyn Small -

8

A Husband's Story

Story Submitted By: Tom Schmidt

In thinking of staying and standing women, the first woman I thought of was my wife, Margaret. Many things that she's done in the course of our life together have been a tremendous source of strength and inspiration to me Much of this I didn't appreciate at the time, but only recently have come to recognize as a wonderful gift. Men try to define themselves and their contribution in life based on the jobs they hold, the money they've made, the things they've accumulated, things that they've done that get the headlines. What has been tremendously inspiring and powerful for me to realize is the tremendous sacrifice that my wife has made over the course of time.

It started early in our marriage. I had just graduated from Marquette University and I was considering graduate school. Margaret had completed one year of college before we were married. We realized that we couldn't afford to both be going to school at the same time. She decided that she would work so that I could obtain my MBA. About mid-way through the MBA program, our oldest daughter was born. I was almost finished with my studies, but now we had a new baby to care for. College once again got put on the back burner for Margaret.

My first job opportunity out of school was on the east coast. Both of our families are in the Midwest and Margaret is very close to her relatives. I thought this would be an adventure for us. I am sure that it was more frightening for Margaret with a newborn baby and not knowing anyone in Connecticut but she was very supportive. She said, "If this is the job that you feel offers the best potential, then let's do it." So we picked up and moved to Connecticut.

The transition was easier for me because of the work environment. I was meeting with people all day long. Margaret was stuck at home with a six-month-old baby in a strange town where she knew no one. After work I would get invited to go golfing or bowling with the guys. Many times this put an additional strain on

Margaret. After taking care of our daughter all day, she forward to getting some help from me in the evenings.

There were times when she became upset with my insensitivity. "Honey, the guys are going golfing after work, you don't mind if I join them, do you?" It put additional pressure on her. It was very hard for her, but she challenged herself to become more outgoing and she made many new friends.

We lived in Connecticut for only two years before we moved back to the Midwest, but I know now that it was tough for Margaret. She was out of her comfort zone but rarely complained. She wasn't looking at the things that she needed. She was doing what she felt needed to be done to support me.

By 1981, we had two daughters and I was working at Northwest Airlines. I was moving up the corporate ladder. Margaret was pregnant with our third child. The day before our son was born, we found out he had a congenital birth defect (a condition known as anencephalia) and he wasn't expected to live more than a few hours after he was born. This was a very tough time for both of us, but tremendously tough for Margaret. There was little support from our friends and relatives, because they didn't know what to say or how to act around us. We felt like we were battling this alone. We also handled it in different ways. Being the typical male, I felt that I needed to have the answer for why this was happening. Of course, I didn't have that answer. So my thoughts were, "Just buck up and move on with our life, act as if it didn't happen, and get back into our daily routine." Margaret had carried our son for 8+ months and wanted to know why this happened. Was it something we did? Was there something we could have done to prevent this? Could this happen again? She wanted to talk to someone about this. She wanted me to be there for her to listen and share her grief.

One of the hardest lessons in life - a lesson that women seem to know instinctively, but men just don't get - is that "being" is more important than "doing". I learned this lesson the hard way through the experience of our son's birth and death. Margaret wanted (and needed) me to be there for her. She was there for me, but I felt that if I didn't have an answer, if I couldn't provide some solutions, explain why this happened, and guarantee that it wouldn't happen again, that I was a failure as a husband. So why dwell on something you can't explain or understand. Let's just marched on. This was a very tough time in our life. Eventually Margaret sat me down and said, "Look. We're either going to talk about this or I'm leaving." I finally realized that Margaret wasn't looking for answers from me. She didn't want me to "do" anything. She just wanted me to be there for her the way she had always been there for me. I had always been under the illusion that as a guy you had to solve the problems or you weren't doing your job. In this situation there were no answers. Our faith played a role in our coping with our son's death, but it was really by helping each other that we made it through. For me, more than anything else, that was the strength of Margaret. Not that she wasn't hurting (far from it), but I saw what staying and standing really meant.

We wanted more children. It took a lot of courage for Margaret to get pregnant, because of what happened to our son, but she did get pregnant. Our third daughter was born happy and healthy. Margaret continued staying at home and caring for the kids. She's always been willing to sacrifice for me and for the kids. I am sure that she will provide the same things for our grandkids.

About a year ago Margaret's mom, who is almost 91, couldn't continue living in the assisted care retirement home where she had been staying. They basically said she required nursing home care. We had little notice and had to move her quickly to a nursing home or provide someone on a 24-hour-a-day basis until we could move her. We decided to move her to our house until we could explore tour options. Margaret disagreed that her mother required nursing home care. She felt that her mom, who was very sharp mentally, just needed help with her physical restrictions. Margaret didn't want to put her mother in a place where she would to be ignored. So Margaret began caring for her mother in our home. Caring for her mother has been physically demanding, but it's something Margaret insists on doing as long as she can. It is an indication of her commitment. She's told me many times, "My mom took care of me when I was little. Until my mom needs more care than I can give her, I will be there for her." Margaret has been there for me, for her mom, for our children, and even our grandchild. She has a tremendous amount of dedication to her family.

Unfortunately this dedication is something I did not always recognize and even took advantage of at times. I have come to realize how truly blessed I am to have Margaret in my life and appreciate her more than I could ever explain. She has shown me what it means to love unconditionally. To me she epitomizes what it means to be a staying and standing woman.

9

A Cancer Journey

Story Submitted by Peg DeVries

My story of the cancer experience started in 1995. That's when I was diagnosed with cancer. I had a lump in my right breast. I had been going to the same breast clinic since I was 36 years old for fibrocystic breasts. I had seen the same doctor for years and years and I can remember him coming into the room after a biopsy. I was with a friend, and he said, "Well, it's cancer". He was very objective and non-emotional.

I followed through with the same doctor through my second episode, which occurred a couple years later. Unfortunately, he initially ignored my concerns. I had been describing pain in my shoulder for some time and he would always say, "Thank God that you're alive." In the fall of '97, I was pressing harder for answers but it took until May '98 to find something definitive. There was a tumor wrapped around a key blood vessel near my collarbone and it was inoperable. The breast cancer that had traveled to this area. I changed doctors at this time.

I was also very angry with the doctor the second time. He wouldn't listen to me. I would tell him at check ups that my shoulder wasn't right. Often my exploratory nature makes me think about what different steps I could have taken. Is the cancer my fault? Is it my fault because I created so much stress for myself? I think that it was but not entirely.

I've always had a lot of support. I have worked with a healing coach. To the healing people, it was easy to reach out. To friends and co-workers, it was harder. To people better in tune to this, it was easier. I think I lost a couple of friends who couldn't cope with this. That made me realize that it was a difficult thing to address in friendship to the degree and level that I needed. Most of my friends are there still and, of course, my family. I have two really good friends at work and three outside of work that I share a lot with and who have supported me.

My psychologist is open to anything I have to share. I understand that it is hard for people. It takes a professional person for me to open to the deepest struggles. My friends are wonderful. My family is wonderful. To really get to the root of the pain, it takes a professional. No matter how caring and loving people are around me, I just don't know if they're the best people to go to.

I believe that for me this is a very singular journey. That's good and bad. It's very character building and it's very strengthening and it's very tough. I reached out to other cancer patients the first two times. I lived for three weeks with all these cancer people when I traveled to Germany for treatment. I'm a very sensitive person. Being with a lot of cancer people can be very overwhelming. I remember a woman that I met at Huteland Clinic. She had cancer very bad and we talked about death.

With some people I get some insights as to why they have the cancer. And that's a little difficult because I feel for them. It is a challenge for me to be with others who have cancer and see them die. I was in Arizona in March. I called some fellow patients from that trip and they had both died. I expected them to die, but still it was surprising that it happened so fast. I have another friend that has advanced cancer and now has a blockage in her gallbladder. I hope I'm not pretending I am different from them. I value being able to function and go on. I think part of my attitude is self-preservation. I feel like my hands are full with my situation and it is difficult to take on other's cancer needs. This time is a singular journey. I know where the support groups are and where help is, but chose to operate in a smaller circle. I have to protect myself and put up boundaries.

I have a long way to go. I have to learn to forgive and let go. And one of the main points is that so much of what we take in is disorienting. I'm still working on myself. I'm trying to take better care of myself. I hope that the path I'm on is helping me. I'm still struggling. The latest undertaking is the whole concept of forgiveness, and really understanding and really doing it. That is very hard for me. I wrestle with the notion of living in the moment. Yet, I'm optimistic and happy with life and who I am.

There have been many forks in the road with the decisions I have had to make. Every time I've had cancer, I've had to make decisions about what I need to do and which way I need to go. It's the most pressing fork of late. I'm at a kind of fork in realizing what matters. That has happened all along during this cancer thing, but it's more pronounced now. Animals, nature and family mean a great deal to me. I have a deepened sense of spirituality. I think when anyone faces the possibility of death that she goes deeper. I've read a lot about the death experience. I have strong instincts, so I haven't felt the need to face the death experience just yet. In a spiritual sense, this is a remarkable journey. To think that I have survived has deepened me. It's remarkable. I feel so fortunate that I had the kinds of treatments and that I've had the ability and interest in being involved in the process. When I think about spirituality, there must be a reason why I'm still here.

10

The Gift Of Pain

Story Submitted By: Kathy Tunheim

One of the biggest stories of my life began in 1998. I was 38 years old and at the time, I had a wonderful position as the Director of Leadership Development at American Express Financial Advisors. It was a good stage in my life, but also a very busy time. Our children were ages 6, 3, and 1. We had just moved into our new home that we had built. My husband was a partner at his law firm. Life was full, but good.

In January of that year, I was responsible for a large, executive development conference in Phoenix for the top sales executives at AEFA. My team and I were running from 6:00 a.m. to midnight as we prepared for this huge event. During the conference, I suddenly developed the worst headache of my life. I had never been a person who experienced migraines, so it was disturbing that the never-ending pounding would not go away. The conference ended and I came home, but I found I could not get rid of this constant headache.

I have described them as "Shazam headaches." One would hit me when I least expected it and would flatten me. I would be driving in a car and I would have to pull over and lay down on the car seat. After I lay down for a while, it went away and I was better. Then I would sit up and drive on to work. Before long, another "Shazam headache" would appear and I would have to lie down at work. I would try to go to my first meeting of the day and I could sometimes last 45-50 minutes until I would get another headache and would have to lie down. It got so ludicrous that I would take a pillow and a blanket to my office and repeated this all day long.

Life was so full and my schedule so busy that I just couldn't find time to get to the doctor. My staff finally made me make the appointment. It seemed like such an interruption to my day! There were all sorts of tests: three MRIs, three CAT scans and a spinal tap. I was concerned that they thought I had brain cancer, which was very frightening. After the spinal tap, they said, "Kathi, you don't have any spinal fluid and we don't know why." At that point, I went to Mayo clinic. The good news was that I didn't have brain cancer but the bad news is that I did have a hole in the dura of my spinal cord. Most of my spinal fluid had leaked into my body. When I would lie down, the little spinal fluid I had left could travel to my brain and erase the headaches. When I sat or stood up, the spinal fluid drained out of my brain cavity and my brain would seize up, which was why I was getting the piercing headaches.

They said that I had two options. The first was very risky surgery because of the potential for paralysis. They could not locate the exact spinal cord opening, so that made it even more risky. The second option was to lay flat in bed for some length of time and see if the spinal cord would heal itself. The Mayo physician looked me right in the eye and said, "I don't know how you got this condition. You don't play football. You haven't been in a car accident. There has been no trauma to your system. The only thing I can surmise is that you need to change your life-style. I think you are carrying a lot of stress and for some reason, your body has decided to carry it in this way. Go home and make some changes. I cannot assure you that you will <u>ever</u> heal and even if you do, the headaches could come back at any time. You may have this condition for the rest of your life."

At 38, suffering with these piercing headaches for the rest of my life sounded awful. I remember looking out the window and seeing my neighbor, LeAnn, playing catch with her two kids. All I wanted to do in life at that time was to be able to play catch with my three kids and husband. Nothing else mattered.

I went home and grew quite depressed. Being in my bedroom 24 hours/day was so unusual. I was accustomed to a day filled with commutes, meetings, kids' events, dinner and more work once everyone else was in bed. I felt like a failure, called my boss and said, "I can't come to work." So I took a leave of absence.

For four of the six months I laid on my back and read, and read, and read. There was this big stack of books next to my bed that I had never found time to read. Now was my opportunity. Amazingly, every one of the books in the stack was about "Finding Work/Life Balance," "The Time Bind," "Putting Family First." The theme was pretty evident.

The biggest surprise to me was the incredible spiritual awakening – almost a personal transformation that began to happen in me. For the first time in my life, I wanted to be still. I wanted to "be" and not "do." I had a desire to meditate, pray and journal in a way I hadn't done in years. I found my way back to my dusty bible and began reading verses in there I'd never seen before. "Come to me, all you who are weary and burdened, and I will give you rest." (Matthew 11:28)

It slowly changed my outlook and approach in my life. Instead of feeling sorry for myself, thinking about "ain't it awful" that this happened to me, I began to thank God for this respite…this badly needed sabbatical that I had been given.

One afternoon, I was lying on the floor of my bedroom in front of the fire, feeling the warmth on a cool, March day, when suddenly this incredible, loud thought permeated my entire being. "Kathi, I have given you many talents and gifts. I want you to take those out of American Express and start sharing your leadership gifts with my church." I couldn't get away from this idea. It kept repeating itself over and over. I grabbed my journal and began to write questions. Why me, Lord? Why can't you ask someone else? What if I fail? I don't want to start my own business right now. We had just built a large house in Orono. I need my big paycheck and bonus from AMEX to make ends meet. Why me, now? The idea continued to repeat itself over and over. There was no mistake here. I knew I was getting told what to do, even if I didn't especially like it or agree with it at this point in time.

Unlike me, instead of jumping into action, I also started to work with a counselor to learn more about my family of origin. Why was I so wired to be a workaholic? Why did I enjoy being at work so much more than at home? Why was the rush of accomplishment higher for me there than anywhere else in my life? I knew I was addicted to work, but I didn't know why. In order for me to heal physically and emotionally, I knew deep down that I had to answer some of these questions.

The counselor asked very simple questions of me and it got clear quickly. I come from a family of farmers on both sides, good people who worked about 24 hours a day, 7 days a week. My parents had owned a fishing and vacationing resort while I was growing up, which also required working about 24 hours a day and 7 days a week. It became clear that I took that same belief system to my places of employment, including American Express, and really enjoyed the "high" of accomplishing things and getting rewarded for hard work. I was addicted to work and had been my entire life.

Having to learn to "be" differently was scary. Being a "workaholic" is all that I knew how to "do." And now leaving

AMEX and perhaps starting my own business was the scariest proposition I'd ever faced…let alone think about the rejection factor! What if no one hired me! We'd lose the house…or worse yet, I'd have to change some of my buying patterns. Walking away from a big corporate salary and perks seemed ludicrous, especially that I enjoyed my work so much. However, thinking about the alternatives and facing more piercing headaches that left me debilitated, I decided that if I did get better, I would entertain the thought of starting my own business.

In four months I did get better. The headaches slowly faded away. In May, I walked a block and realized that I might be normal someday. In June, I walked a mile and realized that I was going to get through this thing. I took the summer off, and had the best summer of my life. I played with my children, went to the beach, spent time at our lake cabin. I finally learned how to play and relax. It may sound strange, but I didn't know how! I started my business in July and fortunately, by September 15, I had been referred to a client by a loving and supportive relative and negotiated a retainer for a nine month project. It was a blast trying new things and helping another organization with my talents and gifts. It was a Lutheran college, a part of His church, just as He said.

Next week I'll celebrate my company's five-year anniversary. It has been the most rewarding five years of my 20-year career! Getting sick was the best thing that could have ever happened to me. In my new life, I get to be a mom, volunteer and professional. I have learned to take care of myself first.

If I don't do that, I am no good to anyone else. So few women understand this concept. I certainly didn't "get it" until I was forced to learn the lesson the hard way.

As someone who had NO work/life balance in her life, I have become quite an expert on the topic. I've read about every book on the topic that I can get my hands on. I speak on the topic two to three times a month now. It looks as though this topic will be my Ph.D. dissertation focus in a few years. This life issue has chosen me. I did not choose it.

It's something I talk about with my clients. Everywhere I look, leaders in corporations, education, government and non-profits, are all struggling with being a productive worker and having a life, too.

My greatest learning from this entire experience is that from out of my greatest pain in life, has come my greatest gift to the world. I am here to serve others with my learning, help them suffer less and appreciate each and every day.

My mission is to appreciate, educate and inspire servant leadership in others to glorify God.

The mission of Tunheim Leadership Group, Inc., is to educate and inspire leadership, team and organizational development in others to help them reach their God-given potential.

CHERYL LEITSCHUH

Dr. Cheryl Leitschuh, Ed.D. assists companies in achieving their key business objectives by fully capitalizing on a single line of their balance sheet - their human resource potential. Cheryl uses powerful programming, assessments and technology to harness and then maximize the untapped potential of a company's human resource assets.

When working with individuals, her typical engagements include developing key leaders and managers, enhancing talent development, developing focus in vision and implementing this vision both personally and professionally. When working with an organization, Dr. Leitschuh addresses the short term and long term business objectives by focusing on human talent development. These projects have focused on conflict resolution, trust management and enhancing team performance.

Cheryl has a broad range of clients that include health care, high tech and professional service firms. One of Dr. Leitschuh's specialties has been to work with professional service firms and their technical professionals -- lawyers, accountants, engineers and consultants.

Dr. Leitschuh is a licensed psychologist and holds a doctorate degree in Educational Psychology and Counseling. Her dissertation was "A Descriptive Study of Mentoring from The Perspective of Mentors in Business and Industry". She speaks on an assortment of topics related to career vision, organizational leadership and enhancing human talent. She is listed in *Who's Who of American Women* and *Who's Who of Professional Women.* She is also a professional member of the National Speaker's Association.

Cheryl Leitschuh & Associates, Inc.
4468 N. Mallard Trail
Eagan, MN 55122
651-398-7151
E-Mail: Cheryl@career-future.com
Web: www.career-future.com

If you have a story you would like to submit for future volumes of <u>Staying and Standing Women</u>, please contact:

Cheryl Leitschuh
651-398-7151
Or
Cheryl@career-future.com

Additional Books Written By
Dr. Cheryl Leitschuh, Ed.D.

Real World Career Development Strategies That Work!!

A power packed collection of insights and strategies from professionals who make a difference each and every day! No theoretical principles here. You get Real-World Strategies from experts who work in the trenches day in and day out.

ORDER FORM

Complete the following order form and mail to Cheryl Leitschuh, 4468 N. Mallard Trail, Eagan, MN 55122.

FREE shipping and handling on all orders. Tax included!
****

____ I would like to order ________ copies of **Staying and Standing Women. 13.95 each**

_____ I would like to order ________ copies of **Real World Career Development Strategies That Work!!** 19.95 each

Total amount enclosed ____________

Ship to:

Name:

Company:

Address:

City: State:

Zip:

Phone:

Email:

Please allow 10-14 days for delivery.

For questions on your order, email Cheryl@career-future.com
Or call 651-398-7151